Must Love Gherkins

Amy Finnegan

Presentation by *BookLeaf Publishing*

Web: www.bookleafpub.com

E-mail: info@bookleafpub.com

ISBN: 9789395969123

First edition 2022

DEDICATION

For James and Riley

My everything

ACKNOWLEDGEMENT

My year 7 teacher once encouraged me to write.

I didn't listen to her, but twenty years later here I am with a messy book of thoughts and scribbles.

So I guess that's something?

Thanks, Mrs. Harrison.

PREFACE

I have no idea what this book is or what it will become.

It is a wholesome journey that we can explore together.

Hello

That perfect ray of light grazes your cheek and
fills your body

The luminous glow radiates from something
within you

I can almost touch the feeling as it engulfs you

We are so different, but could be be the same?

Hello

You

Of everyone I've ever loved
There's a special spot for you
You showed me what it really meant and shared
it right back too

You never did question us or what we may
become
You dove right it, intoxicated, sober all in one

As time collects it's moments and adds in people
too
The thing that never changes is the love I feel
for you

Remember, if there ever is a day that seems too
tough
Nothing in this whole wide world is built as
strong as us

Love

It was when we'd drive to nowhere
It was when we'd sit in silence
It was when we talked about our dreams
It was when you held me close

It was when you shared your darkness
It was when you gave me light
It was when you were my person
It was when you wore white

It was when you support me
It was when we created life
It was when we fight
And it was everyday since

Shadow

How easy it is to say
Good, yes, I'm fine
How quick we are to hide
Our smile screams
Alone, surrounded by people

Don't fear
Our vulnerability bonds us
Side by side we travel
My darkness and your light
Together
Always

Creation

The flood of joy
Then the worry and pain
The distorted views and feelings of loneliness

Will we be okay?
Will I be enough?
This little seeds waiting
Do not give up

The flower has grown
It's in full bloom
The moment has come
To birth life
Create

Son

There is a moment
A pause
All emotions are felt; an explosion within

It's time
Creation of new
Two souls from one
A mother and son

Star

How proud you should be
Of the man that you are
So caring, so gentle
Beyond years, by far

You have your own bubble
You like your own space
But all that love and emotion exudes every place

Your mind is unique
Your thoughts so refined
Your focus and curiosity is one of a kind

Your patience
Your kindness
Can not be learned
What you hold in your heart is yours that you've
earned

As you continue along this path you have made
The stars shine bright, may they never fade

Mountains

Never has there ever been a soul as free as you
I have to take a breath to appreciate that too
Your excitement, your energy so raw and
igniting
Such independence and fierceness, at times may
be frightening

I cannot put into words how much joy and life
you make
I didn't realise then but my soul is now awake

Your thirst and wonder is infectious
Your knowledge before your time
My little bundle of energy
Mountains you will climb

Bestfriend

The door has been dormant for an eternity
Suspense lingers
A stillness in the air
Protection is demanded of us

Noise
Motion
The time has come
An overwhelming sigh of relief
A creek followed by anticipation

A gush of joy erupts from within
The excitement impossible to contain
When will she say it?
When will she say it?

'Who's been a good boy?'

Power

Make your words tremble
The power they demand
Expelled from your body
With courage

May your core tighten
And rage fill the pit inside
For today you speak free of judgement

Today is everyday
Use your voice
Be heard
Silence is lifeless

Your World

You explore your world so gently
Perfectly delicate
What a blissful place
I want to be in your world
I want to see your world
Why do we loose sight as we grow
We must continue to see your world
We must keep your world alive

Day One

Checkered, collared, pristine
Dark, unknown
The light beaming, unforgivingly
The safety in the shadows
Choice
Glowing
Your light is blinding

Unforgiving

Do not keep time waiting
Time is unforgiving
It will not say what needs to be said before you
lay your head
The needed words, waiting there before your
pillow warms
It will not venture and explore the dream your
soul craves
It brushes your cheeks with the wind
Moments worth waiting for do not need a ticket
Say those words
Make that change
Be unapologetically present and ready
Do not wait for that moment

Within

My beautiful boy
So gentle, so kind
What will this place do to you?
Swallowing your light until the shadows
embrace you?
When you feel the darkness come, look within,
you are the spark that self ignites

Daughter

Rest your weary head upon my shoulder
Forever there it will be
No need for words or permission
I will never change the key

For one day when the ground you stand isn't as
stable as you would like
The door it always open
Ajar, day or night

As we sit in silence
Together we will grow
You may not need it all the time
But it will never, ever go

One day you will find a new safe place and
receive the love you deserve
But far beyond the fateful date my daughters
spots reserved

My Person

No matter where I am in this world
I'm always drawn to you
Even with my busy mind
You always jump the queue

Your thinking stare
You're stubbled face
The breath that leaves your lips,
So everlasting on my mind
My heart, a beat it skips

Why?

What's the point of the sun if it's too bright to
see?
What's the point of love if you don't love me?

This was my first poem I wrote when I was 11
years old. I now understand the value of the sun.

Sunshine

With each rainy day
A bright rainbow comes to play
How lucky we are

www.ingramcontent.com/pod-product-compliance
Lightning Source LLC
Chambersburg PA
CBHW060930130726
48001CB00006B/2500

9 789339 596912 3